BECOMING
A WOMAN WHO
$\mathcal{L}$OVES

BECOMING A WOMAN WHO LOVES

"A new commandment I give to you, that you love one another; as I have loved you, that you also love one another."

John 13:34 NKJV

A BIBLE STUDY BY

CYNTHIA HEALD

OLIVER NELSON ™

THOMAS NELSON PUBLISHERS®
Nashville

A Division of Thomas Nelson, Inc.
www.ThomasNelson.com

Published in Nashville, Tennessee, by Thomas Nelson, Inc.

Published in association with the literary agency of Alive Communications, Inc., 7680 Goddard St., Suite 200, Colorado Springs, CO 80920.

Unless otherwise indicated, all Scripture quotations are taken from the *King James Version* of the Bible.

Scripture quotations noted MESSAGE are from *The Message: The New Testament in Contemporary English*. Copyright © 1993 by Eugene H. Peterson; and *The Message: The Wisdom Books*. Copyright © 1996 by Eugene H. Peterson. Used by permission of NavPress, Box 6000, Colorado Springs, CO 80934.

Scripture quotations noted NKJV are from THE NEW KING JAMES VERSION. Copyright © 1979, 1980, 1982, Thomas Nelson, Inc., Publishers.

Scripture quotations noted NLT are from *The Holy Bible*, New Living Translation, copyright © 1996. Used by permission of Tyndale House Publishers, Inc., Wheaton, Illinios, 60189. All rights reserved.

Scripture quotations noted PHILLIPS are from J.B. Phillips: THE NEW TESTAMENT IN ENGLISH, Revised Edition. Copyright © J.B. Phillips 1958, 1960, 1972. Used by permission of Macmillan Publishing Co., Inc.

Scripture quotations noted WILLIAMS are from *The New Testament in the Language of the People*, by Charles Williams. Copyright © 1986 by Holman Bible Publishers. All rights reserved.

ISBN 0-7852-7243-7

Printed in the United States of America

04 05 PHX 8 7

$\mathcal{C}$ONTENTS

How to Use This Guide

This Bible study has been created to help you search the Scriptures and draw closer to God as you seek to grow in Christlike love. All you need is a Bible, a writing tool, and an expectant heart. You may find it helpful, however, to have access to supplemental resources such as a Bible translation in addition to the one you normally use, a general dictionary, a general Bible commentary, a Bible handbook, or a study Bible with reference notations.

Becoming a Woman Who Loves is appropriate for individual as well as group use, and for women of any age and season of life. Before you begin each chapter, pray for attentiveness to how God is speaking to you through His Word and for sensitivity to His prompting. At the conclusion of each chapter, you will have the opportunity to write out whatever God may be prompting you to learn, or reflect on, or apply. Ask God to direct your response to this personalized question so that you might receive His abundant love for you, which will in turn supply the love you give to others. Adding Scripture memorization to this practice will help you abide in the love of Christ, the True Vine, day by day.

Quotations from Christian writers are included to help you understand the biblical content of each chapter and to enhance your personal response to God's Word. Consider using the "Notes" section in the back of this book as a resource list for further devotional reading and study.

The Bible has much to say about the importance of learning from and encouraging one another in the community of believers. If you are using this study with a small group, the questions and exercises that are provided will give you excellent opportunities for talking and praying together about loving one another as Christ loves you.

REFACE

While reading in the gospel of John, I was struck with the command that Jesus gave to His disciples on the night of His betrayal. He was sharing His last words with His band of men—important, significant words to be remembered and taken to heart. "A new commandment I give to you, that you love one another; as I have loved you, that you also love one another. By this all will know that you are My disciples, if you have love for one another" (John 13:34–35 NKJV).

As I read these words, I thought, *What is the old commandment? The old commandment is to love my neighbor as I love myself.* As I considered the old and new commands, I realized that I liked the old commandment better! The new commandment raised the standard for loving. *I think it is easier to love others as I love myself,* I thought. *How could I possibly love as Jesus loved? He loved sacrificially, unconditionally, and passionately. He forgave, He was patient, He didn't mind being interrupted.*

I was challenged with the thought of studying the implications of this new commandment. Could I really learn to love as Jesus loved? What exactly would this love look like? Could I actually grow in this love so that it would become a part of my daily life? What would this godly love cost me?

With no little hesitancy, I began to study how to become a woman who loves. I knew it would not be easy, and in fact it has been incredibly convicting. But it has also been life changing. Any time love is pursued, the pursuer can never be the same, for it is the nature of love to transform.

As a result of this study, my understanding of love has broadened. Now I realize how critical godly love is to the body of Christ and to the world around us. I have been challenged to come before the Lord selflessly and willingly, allowing Him to teach me to grow continually in love.

Christ desires that all His disciples love one another with His love. My prayer is that as you take time to study and pray over the Scriptures and questions we discuss, you will become a woman who loves the Lord and others wholeheartedly and passionately.

My benediction is the same as Paul's to the Thessalonians: "May the Lord make your love grow and overflow to each other and to everyone else, just as our love overflows toward you. As a result, Christ will make your hearts strong, blameless, and holy when you stand before God our Father . . ." (1 Thess. 3:12–13 NLT).

In His love,

Cynthia Heald

So, chosen by God for this new life of love, dress in the wardrobe God picked out for you: compassion, kindness, humility, quiet strength, discipline. Be even-tempered, content with second place, quick to forgive an offense. Forgive as quickly and completely as the Master forgave you. And regardless of what else you put on, wear love. It's your basic, all-purpose garment. Never be without it.

Colossians 3:12–14 MESSAGE

The Father and the Child

The Father spoke:

My child, do you know that I love you?

Yes, Father, I know that You love me.

How do you know of My love?

You sent Your Son to die on the cross for my sins. You have adopted me as Your own child. You have given me Your Holy Spirit who has transformed my heart with Your love.

Since you have freely received My love, do you freely love others?

I try, Father, but I do not love perfectly.

My child, I want you to be intent on learning to love as I love you. It is of paramount importance to Me.

Yes, Father. I want to do only what You desire. Here is my heart—it is Yours. Fill it with Your love and do what is necessary to teach me to love.

CHAPTER 1

THE
SUPREMACY OF LOVE

❦

There are three things that will endure—
faith, hope, and love—and the greatest of
these is love.

1 Corinthians 13:13 NLT

Love is the most God-like state of the soul. God is not faith or hope; <u>God is love</u>. The Eternal does not believe or anticipate, but he does love—he is love. Love is the life of the soul. It warms every vein and beats in every pulse.[1]

David Thomas

*I*n his first letter to the church at Corinth, the apostle Paul addressed a group of believers who were preoccupied with seeking and practicing the most prominent spiritual gifts. To help them maintain a balanced perspective, Paul encouraged the Corinthians to pursue "a more excellent way" (1 Cor. 12:31 NKJV). The best way to minister to the body of Christ, he concluded, was to exercise the supreme virtue of love. Although he acknowledged the lasting value of faith and hope, even these would one day be eclipsed. For Paul to single out one virtue as the greatest, above all others, indicates that he had a firm conviction based on his own experience and his certainty of the heart of God. Categorically and boldly, he proclaimed that the highest, the loveliest, the preeminent virtue of all is love.

The Prominence of Love

1. To discover the heart of God and what He desires most for His children, we can examine His Word. What central theme is taught in each of the following Scriptures?

   a. Mark 12:28–31

b. Romans 13:8–9

c. 1 Corinthians 13:13

d. 1 Corinthians 16:14

2. Of all the commands in the Bible and among all the great virtues, love reigns supreme. What do these passages communicate about why love is God's priority?

a. Romans 13:10

b. 1 Corinthians 8:1–3

c. Colossians 3:14

3. Our culture has given us many popular songs and sayings about the importance and beauty of love. List some of your favorite song titles or quotations, and then describe what kind of love is prized in our society.

Love being the most potent of forces, it is hardly surprising that the most overwhelming experiences of life should be those of being in love—first with God and then with another human being. There is no trick or a magician or spell of a witchdoctor, no drug or mesmerism or bribery or torture or coercion that can compare in power with the force for change unleashed in the human breast through the touch of love. Love is the greatest of teachers, for there is no authority more compelling, no power more hypnotically transfixing, no counsel more wise, no message we are more longing to hear, no other master for whom it is easier to give up absolutely everything in order to follow and obey.[2]

Mike Mason

The Highest Love

4. The world tends to glorify relational and physical love. But the greatest love, which Paul extols, is from a rarely used word in the Greek language, *agapē*. It describes "a love that is based on the deliberate choice of the one who loves rather than the worthiness of the one who is loved."[3] How do the following verses characterize this kind of love?

a. Psalm 145:8–9

b. Jeremiah 31:3

c. John 3:16–17

d. 1 Corinthians 13:4–7

God, who needs nothing, loves into existence wholly superfluous creatures in order that He may love and perfect them . . . If I may dare the biological image, God is a "host" who deliberately creates His own parasites; causes us to be that we may exploit and "take advantage of" Him. Herein is love. This is the diagram of Love Himself, the inventor of all loves.[4]

C. S. Lewis

5. Agapē love is self-sacrificing, desiring the best for another. How has God demonstrated this kind of love to the world?

How has His unconditional love shaped your life?

Author's Reflection

Some of my favorite old love songs are by Irving Berlin: "I'll Be Loving You Always" and "How Deep Is the Ocean." I grew up listening to Elvis Presley sing, "Love Me Tender," and many times I would find myself humming, "What the World Needs Now Is Love, Sweet Love." Browning's poetic stanza, "How do I love thee? Let me count the ways," Tennyson's declaration, "It is better to have loved and lost, than never to have loved at all," and the saying, "Love makes the world go round" captured my attention as a young girl.

I remember watching the Academy Awards one year when a movie actress was so overcome with emotion as she received an Oscar that she repeatedly cried, "You *like* me!" It is, indeed, a precious gift to be loved, wanted, and accepted.

Throughout history the incalculable value of love has been proclaimed in every art form and culture—personally, privately, and publicly. Certainly the Scriptures address the whole scope of love. Sexual love in the context of marriage is blessed by God, love between friends is prized, and agapē love is presented as the highest and best to achieve.

C. S. Lewis offers a unique insight into this special agapē love when he portrays God as the host who actively invites and welcomes His "parasitic" children to cling to and depend upon Him. The connotation of the word *parasite* is usually negative, because a parasite can ultimately destroy its host. There are, however, a few positive synonyms for the word *parasite*—"follower" and "attendant"—which perfectly describe those who choose to hold fast to the Lord God. Far from destroying this loving Host, God's children bring Him pleasure when they acknowledge and accept His kind invitation to be fed, protected, and nurtured by Him.

God has demonstrated the highest love for in Christ's sacrifice, He has accepte His dependent followers unconditionally. In this beautiful context of agapē love, the "parasite" embraces faith, experiences hope, and receives eternal life. What an extremely gracious Host is our God, who generously imparts His love to all who desire to live with Him. In loving and clinging to Him, we can experience the greatest love that life has to offer.

We know but little now about the conditions of the life that is to come. But what is certain is that love must last. God, the Eternal God, is love. Covet, therefore, that everlasting gift, that one thing which it is certain is going to stand, that one coinage which will be current in the universe when all the other coinages of all the nations of the world shall be useless and unhonored. You will give yourself to many things; give yourself first to love.[5]

Henry Drummond

Love Imparted

6. As you review this chapter, ask the Lord what He wants you to learn concerning the supremacy of love. Is there a verse on which you need to meditate or a teaching about which you need to pray so that love can begin to dwell in your heart in a more powerful way? Write down your thoughts and pray for God's love to invade your heart and teach you about what you personally need to become a woman who loves.

⁌ Scripture Memory Verse:

1 Corinthians 13:13

"But now faith, hope, love, abide these three; but the greatest of these is love.

CHAPTER 2

A New Commandment

❧

So now I am giving you a new commandment: Love each other. Just as I have loved you, you should love each other. Your love for one another will prove to the world that you are my disciples.

John 13:34–35 NLT

So a new a type of love is given that, as the Greek expositors generally have urged, there is a deeper intensity in the love than can be found in the Mosaic principle, "Love thy neighbour as thyself." In this commandment, which embraces the whole law, self-love is assumed, and is made the standard for the love of neighbour. This [command], on the other hand, would be based on a new principle, and measured by a higher standard, and even mean more than love of self altogether. Christ's love to his disciples was self-abandoning, self-sacrificing love.[1]

H. R. Reynolds

A few hours before Jesus was betrayed, He was with His disciples in the Upper Room. After Jesus had washed their feet, they sat down to eat. During the course of the meal, Jesus predicted that one of them would betray Him. Soon after this pronouncement, Judas left the room, and Jesus spoke these words to those who remained: "Dear children, how brief are these moments before I must go away and leave you!... So now I am giving you a new commandment..." (John 13:33–34 NLT). Only on His last night with His disciples did Jesus share this new directive. On the eve of leaving His faithful followers, His final words took on the utmost importance. In essence He was saying, "You've been with Me for three years, and you know the commands given from Moses, but now as I depart I am giving you a new commandment. Listen to it carefully, because <u>this command is essential for the establishment and unity of the church and for your witness to the world</u>."

If we love only as the world does, we will not be offering hope to the world.

A Sacrificial Love

1. Jesus raised the standard concerning how we are to love one another. He left a model of how to love, and He asks that His disciples love in the same way. As you read the verses below, record how Jesus exemplified the heart of love.

   a. Ephesians 5:1–2
   Be imitators

12

b. Philippians 2:5–8

c. 1 Peter 2:18–25

d. 1 John 3:16

2. Jesus constantly demonstrated His love for others. As you read the following passages, write down your observations in the columns provided, stating how and to whom Jesus showed compassion.

Scripture	Who Was Involved?	What Did Jesus Do?
a. Matthew 9:35-38		
b. Matthew 15:32–37		

Scripture	*Who Was Involved?*	*What Did Jesus Do?*
c. John 8:1–12		
d. John 13:1–17		

Perhaps most humbling of all Jesus' compassionate acts before Calvary was the foot-washing episode in the upper room, recorded in John 13:3–15. This event occurred just prior to the command to love one another. It is difficult for us to comprehend the Lord of Heaven taking on the role of a servant, but he did what was customary in Eastern homes for servants to do—wash the dusty feet of guests. One would assume that others of the group should have offered to perform this service. But Jesus' love was on display in this act of humility. . . . He gave himself completely to them. He could have demanded his rights and could have called on one of them to perform this humbling service, but he chose to serve them. And, remarkably, he chose to include Judas, who had already sold out to the devil.[2]

William M. Fletcher

3. Jesus not only asked the disciples in the Upper Room to love as He loved, but He asks us to do the same. How do you react to being asked to love as Jesus loves?

Loving Others

4. The new command focuses on a specific group of people. In the following passages, Jesus speaks to His disciples and John writes to the church. What are their instructions regarding *how* and *whom* to love?

a. John 13:34–35

b. 1 John 4:7

5. Jesus teaches that there are others we are to love. What do these Scriptures tell us about who else we are to love and how we are to relate to them?

a. Luke 6:27–36

b. Luke 10:25–37

To be a disciple means that we deliberately identify ourselves with God's interests in other people. "That ye love one another, as I have loved you..." the expression of Christian character is not good doing, but Godlikeness. If the Spirit of God has transformed you within, you will exhibit Divine characteristics in your life, not good human characteristics. *God's* life in us expresses itself as God's life, not as a human life trying to be godly.[3]

Oswald Chambers

6. One recurring theme that Jesus modeled and emphasized in His teaching on love is the idea of sacrificially laying down one's life for friends and others. What are some ways of laying down one's life for the good of someone else?

Author's Reflection

It is significant that John 13 begins with the statement, "Before the Passover celebration, Jesus knew that his hour had come to leave this world and return to his Father. He now showed the disciples the full extent of his love" (v. 1 NLT). His first act in *showing the full extent of His love* was to wash their feet. His last act was dying on the cross for our redemption. Jesus was humbly willing to offer Himself as a servant, obediently sacrificing Himself for others (friends or enemies), graciously demonstrating His love to the full extent. To love as Jesus loved is to keep a towel wrapped around our waists so that we are ready to bow down and serve as needed.

One day I went into the kitchen to prepare a cup of tea, and I asked my husband if he wanted some too. He thought for a moment and then replied, "Actually, I'd like a cup of hot chocolate." Standing at the stove (without a "towel" around my waist) I replied, "Well, hon, if you want hot chocolate, you'll have to fix it yourself. I only have time to make tea."

All of a sudden I had become a Levite rushing down the road past a man in need—with no time in my schedule for anything extra. Sure, I would serve, but only when it was convenient and as long as it didn't interrupt my agenda. Certainly, Jack was not lying beside the road wounded, but my response to him mirrored the attitude of the priest in our Lord's parable of the Good Samaritan.

This new commandment is hard! I've told the Lord that I really like the old commandment better. As hard as the old command is, the new one is a continual challenge—to love sacrificially, humbly, and selflessly. To love in this way, I must always be conscious of the "towel." For me, putting on the towel means surrendering my heart to do whatever the Lord asks, and then being watchful, ready to love and to serve whoever crosses my path. The towel should be so much a part of my life that I "wear" it always, a reminder to give the full extent of my love just as Jesus did.

"A cup of hot chocolate? Certainly! Coming right up."

We instinctively know that love leads to commitment, so we look away when we see a beggar. We might have to pay if we look too closely and care too deeply. Loving means losing control of our schedule, our money, and our time. When we love we cease to be the master and become a servant.[4]

Paul E. Miller

Love Imparted

7. As you review this chapter, ask the Lord what He wants you to learn concerning Jesus' new commandment. Is there a verse on which you need to meditate or a teaching about which you need to pray so that love can begin to dwell in your heart in a more powerful way? Write down your thoughts and pray for God's love to invade your heart and teach you about what you personally need to become a woman who loves.

 Scripture Memory Verses:
John 13:34–35

CHAPTER 3

THE
SOURCE OF LOVE

❧

God showed how much he loved us by sending
his only Son into the world so that we might
have eternal life through him. This is real
love. It is not that we loved God, but that he
loved us and sent his Son as a sacrifice to take
away our sins. Dear friends, since God loved
us that much, we surely ought to love each
other.

1 John 4:9–11 NLT

The springs of love are in God, not in us. It is absurd
to look for the love of God in our hearts naturally; it
is only there when it has been shed abroad in our
hearts by the Holy Spirit.[1]

Oswald Chambers

The new commandment to love as Jesus loved us is a compelling charge—a daunting challenge that seems almost impossible to fulfill. I am not naturally compassionate. I don't see that I have any extra time to give to the wounded by the roadside. I don't like being interrupted, something that happened to Jesus all the time. He loved the lost, the sinful, the grieving. He fed people and washed dusty feet. Am I supposed to do this too? After all, He was God Incarnate; how can I be expected to love as He did? But because I have received God's love, I will be able to love with *His* love. This is the way God provides for those who desire to obey His commands. Thankfully, all our springs find their source in Him.

God's Love to Us

1. Loving others sacrificially is not something we can do in our own strength. What do the following verses communicate about God's love for us and how we can receive it?

a. Romans 5:5–11

b. Ephesians 2:4–7

c. 1 John 4:7–16

2. Once we receive Jesus Christ as our Savior and Lord, our lives are transformed. What do these verses teach about some of the changes that occur when the Holy Spirit fills our hearts with His love?

    a. 2 Corinthians 5:14–17

    b. Ephesians 3:14–19

    c. 1 Peter 1:22–23

Without Christ we should not know God, we could not call upon Him, nor come to Him. But without Christ we also would not know our brother, nor could we come to him. The way is

blocked by our ego. Christ opened up the way to God and to our brother. Now Christians can live with one another in peace; they can love and serve one another; they can become one. But they can continue to do so only by way of Jesus Christ. Only in Jesus Christ are we one, only through Him are we bound together. To eternity He remains the one Mediator.[2]

Dietrich Bonhoeffer

3. Personally accepting Jesus' sacrifice on the cross ushers in new spiritual birth; old things pass away. Describe some of the ways in which your acceptance of Christ has changed your life.

God's Love in Us

4. Once God's love is shed abroad in our hearts, the Holy Spirit begins to work in our lives. What insights can you find in these passages about how God empowers us in learning to love?

a. John 17:20–26

b. Philippians 2:13

c. 1 Thessalonians 3:12–13

d. 1 Thessalonians 4:9–10

5. God is at work in us to conform us to the image of Christ (Rom. 8:29), but it is necessary that we have responsive hearts. What do the following verses tell us about how we are to grow in love?

a. John 14:21–24

b. John 15:9–10

c. 1 John 5:1–3

When God hath given us of his own Spirit and love, so that we in our measure come to love like God, then we know that "we dwell in him, and he in us." There is a loving and abiding intercommunion. We, being in full sympathy with God, must needs yearn to pour forth ourselves to others, as God hath given himself to us. And this outgoing of ourselves to our brother is a sure pledge of God being in us, and we in him.[3]

C. Clemance

6. It is encouraging to know that the Lord is at work in our lives teaching us to love. How does this knowledge affect your attitude toward loving others?

Author's Reflection

One of my favorite hymns is Charles Wesley's "And Can It Be That I Should Gain?" Wesley writes, "Died He for me, who caused His pain? For me, who Him to death pursued? Amazing love! How can it be that Thou, my God, shouldst die for me?"[4] When the full extent of God's love for me begins to flood my life, I realize that God's love is not only amazing but over-

THE SOURCE OF LOVE

whelming. The great love He demonstrated at the cross on my behalf humbles me and draws me to Himself. How can I ever adequately express my gratitude?

I think Jesus tells me simply, "Cynthia, the love that I have given you, I want you to give to others. You are not to try to love with the little love that dwells in your heart, but if you will keep My commands, then I will manifest Myself to you, and I will teach you and cause you to abound in love. Stay close to the source. It is My love that I want you to impart. I'm not asking you to do something that is impossible. In fact, what I'm asking you to do is really simple: accept the love I have for you; allow Me to live in you so that I can teach you how to love. Let Me fill you with My love, My life, My power. In this way you will begin to experience the incomparable blessing of knowing Me and what it is really like to love as I love."

"My dear, dear friends, if God loved us like this, we certainly ought to love each other" (1 John 4:11 MESSAGE).

From God's other known attributes we may learn much about His love. We can know, for instance, that because God is self-existent, His love had no beginning; because He is eternal, His love can have no end; because He is infinite, it has no limit; because He is holy, it is the quintessence of all spotless purity; because He is immense, His love is an incomprehensibly vast, bottomless, shoreless sea before which we kneel in joyful silence and from which the loftiest eloquence retreat confused and abashed.[5]

A. W. Tozer

Love Imparted

7. As you review this chapter, ask the Lord what He wants you to learn concerning the source of your love. Is there a verse on which you need to meditate or a teaching about which you need to pray so that His love can begin to dwell in your heart in a more powerful way? Write down your thoughts and pray for God's love to invade your heart and teach you about what you personally need to become a woman who loves.

 Scripture Memory Verses:
1 John 4:9–11

CHAPTER 4

$\mathcal{B}$EARING $\mathcal{F}$RUIT

❧

*I am the vine, you are the branches. He who
abides in Me, and I in him, bears much
fruit; for without Me you can do nothing.*
                              John 15:5 NKJV

His purpose is not that you will do more for Him but
that you will choose to be more with Him. Only by
abiding can you enjoy the most rewarding friendship
with God and experience the greatest abundance for
His glory.

To abide means to remain, to stay closely connected, to settle in for the long term. With this picture
Jesus is showing the disciples how an ongoing, vital connection with Him will directly determine the amount of
His supernatural power at work in their lives.[1]

Bruce Wilkinson

*J*esus depicted Himself as the Vine, the source from which His followers draw strength, nourishment, and the ability to bear fruit. In describing believers as branches, Jesus portrayed a living and lasting relationship of commitment to Him. It was in this context of abiding that He repeated the new commandment, to love one another as He has loved us (John 15:12). The best choice we can make in order to fulfill this commandment is to stay closely connected to Him. The result of abiding is the precious fruit of Christlikeness. If we do not abide in Him, Jesus makes it clear that we can do nothing—we will bear no fruit and we will eventually wither into lifelessness. To love the Lord and keep His commands, abiding is essential.

The Flesh and the Spirit

1. The choices and decisions we make daily determine the kind of fruit that our lives will produce. Fill in the columns below as you read these passages concerning fruit bearing.

Scripture	Fruit of Our Sinful Nature	Fruit of the Holy Spirit
a. Galatians 5:16–26		
b. Ephesians 5:1–10		

Scripture	Fruit of Our Sinful Nature	Fruit of the Holy Spirit
c. James 3:13–18		

In the flesh, or our depraved nature, there is lust or desire for sinful gratification in some form or another. How are we to be delivered from this, so that it shall not be fulfilled? The way is positively to follow the leading of the Spirit. The idea is not that we are to follow the tendencies of our renewed nature. That is missing the *personal* aspect of the leading. The Spirit, indeed, renews the nature, and excites within it holy desires which seek for gratification. But the Spirit gives personal guiding, especially in and by the reason and conscience in connection with the Word. And as a Guide he is all-sufficient. He is an internal Guide. He throws all the light that we need upon the character of desires and actions, upon the path of duty.[2]

R. Finlayson

2. Certainly the flesh lusts against the Spirit. What insight and encouragement to walk in the Spirit can you find in these verses concerning our old sin nature?

a. Romans 8:1–5

b. Galatians 5:24–25

c. Colossians 3:1–5

To be dead to a thing is a strong expression denoting that it has no influence over us. A man that is dead is uninfluenced and unaffected by the affairs of this life. He is insensible to sounds, and tastes, and pleasures; to the hum of business, to the voice of friendship, and to all the scenes of commerce, gaiety, and ambition. When it is said, therefore, that a Christian is *dead to sin*, the sense is, that it has lost its influence over him; he is not subject to it; he is in regard to that, as the man in the grave is to the busy scenes and cares of this life.[3]

Albert Barnes

3. The Scriptures exhort us to be wise and understanding. How would you summarize the most important truths we need to understand and apply in our lives in order to produce the spiritual fruit of love?

The Vine and the Branches

4. When Jesus was sharing with His disciples on His last night, He left them (and us) a clear picture of what is necessary to be His follower and to bear fruit. You have already read parts of John 15, but there is much in this chapter that can be studied from different perspectives. Read John 15:1–17, and write down the ways in which Jesus' use of the vine imagery teaches us about bearing the fruit of love.

5. Jesus taught that a branch cannot bear fruit by itself. Describe any times in your life when you have tried to bear the fruit of love without abiding in Christ.

Author's Reflection

Few words have had more impact in my life than Jesus' statement, "apart from Me you can do nothing." Many years ago, after meditating on John 15:5, I thought, "I don't want to spend my life doing nothing, so if it takes abiding to do *something*, then that is what I'll do for the rest of my life." Struggling with the busyness of life and my own selfish desires, I have tried to be a branch that remains in the Vine. For me, staying connected to Christ means prayerfully reading His Word daily, memorizing key verses that I really need, and having an ongoing dialogue with the living God throughout the day.

One thing I've learned is that consistent abiding enables me to persevere through pruning—a necessary tool for fruit bearing. Having to let go of dreams, people, the demands of my flesh, and my poor strategies for living are all a part of pruning. Pruning is thinning out, removing, detaching, cleansing—all of it to help me develop and become a sturdy branch, strongly rooted in and connected to the Vine. As I mature, my desire is to draw more and more nourishment from the Lord, to grow in intimacy, and, I hope, to begin to bear much fruit in my desire to love as He loved.

In practical terms, fruit represents good works—a thought, attitude, or action of ours that God values because it glorifies Him. The fruit from your life is how God receives His due honor on earth. That's why Jesus declares, "By this My Father is glorified, that you bear much fruit" (John 15:8).

You bear inner fruit when you allow God to nurture in you a new, Christlike quality: "the fruit of the Spirit is love, joy, peace, longsuffering, kindness, goodness, faithfulness, gentleness, self-control" (Gal. 5:22).

You bear outward fruit when you allow God to work through you to bring Him glory.[4]

Bruce Wilkinson

Love Imparted

6. As you review this chapter, ask the Lord what He wants you to learn concerning bearing the fruit of abiding. Is there a verse on which you need to meditate or a teaching about which you need to pray so that His love can begin to dwell in your heart in a more powerful way? Write down your thoughts and pray for God's love to invade your heart and teach you about what you personally need to become a woman who loves.

 Scripture Memory Verse:
John 15:5

CHAPTER 5

THE CHARACTER
OF LOVE

❦

*Love is patient and kind. Love is not jealous
or boastful or proud or rude. Love does not
demand its own way. Love is not irritable,
and it keeps no record of when it has been
wronged. It is never glad about injustice but
rejoices whenever the truth wins out. Love
never gives up, never loses faith, is always
hopeful, and endures through every
circumstance.*

1 Corinthians 13:4–7 NLT

Love is the badge and character of Christianity.[1]

Donald S. Whitney

*I*n the renowned chapter 13 of Paul's first letter to the Corinthian church, we find the beautiful, challenging, and extraordinary description of love. It is in defining the "more excellent way" that Paul specifically characterizes the many facets of love. After reading this passage, we come away realizing that love is no longer an ethereal concept that only gives us "warm fuzzies". The Word depicts love in all its earthly reality. This love reacts and responds to relationships and circumstances on a distinctively spiritual plane. This love will outlast all spiritual gifts. This love is not hypocritical or self-serving. This love is from above, given to us to put into practice in our world. It is to be so evident that all who meet us will experience its outworking. It is to be the badge of the Christian.

Love Defined

1. Throughout history, many people have attempted to define love. Study Paul's bold statements in 1 Corinthians 13:1–3. Why do you think that the exercise of spiritual gifts and acts of sacrificial service are worth nothing from God's perspective if they are done without love?

THE CHARACTER OF LOVE

2. To create a character sketch of love and its opposite, list all the words Paul uses in 1 Corinthians 13:4–5 to define what love *is* and what love is *not*. Use a dictionary and at least one other Bible translation to define these qualities.

    a. Love *is* . . .

    b. Love *is not* . . .

3. Which of the qualities Paul lists in 1 Corinthians 13:4–5 do you most appreciate in others, and why?

Love suffers for a long time. Our modern "throw-away" society encourages us to get rid of people in our lives who are difficult to get along with, whether they are friends, family or acquaintances. Yet this attitude runs in complete contrast to the love described by Paul. True love puts up with people who would be easier to give up on.[2]

4. Paul further defines love in 13:6–7 by how it is expressed. Record these distinguishing characteristics.

    a. Love *does not:*

    b. Love *does:*

5. Which of these characteristics in 1 Corinthians 13:6–7 challenges you the most in expressing love, and why?

6. After describing the character of love in the first seven verses of chapter 13, Paul shifts to the transcendent nature of love. In verses 8–13, he clarifies that the spiritual gifts, practical as they are to the body of Christ, are temporal. Read 1 Corinthians 13:8–13 and summarize the case Paul makes for love being the "more excellent way" (see 12:31).

> The argument is, that we ought not to seek so anxiously that which is so imperfect and obscure, and which must soon vanish away; but we should rather seek that love which is permanent, expanding, and eternal.[3]
>
> *Albert Barnes*

7. Paul's exhortation depicts the transforming nature of love. Take a moment to examine how this Christlike love is becoming evident in your life. What specific quality in your character needs the most work?

Authors' Reflection

"Thy Love"
The love that gives
no thought to *me,*
but willingly yields
its all to Thee—
O Lord, bestow
deep in my heart
Thy gracious love
ne'er to depart.

—Cynthia Heald

How many of you will join me in reading this chapter (1 Corinthians 13) once a week for the next three months? A man did that once and it changed his whole life. Will you do it? It is for the greatest thing in the world. You might begin by reading it every day, especially the verses which describe the perfect character. "Love suffereth long, and is kind; love envieth not; love vaunteth not itself." Get these ingredients into your life. Then everything that you do is eternal. It is worth doing. It is worth giving time to. No man can become a saint in his sleep; and to fulfill the condition required demands a certain amount of prayer and meditation and time, just as improvement in any direction, bodily or mental, requires preparation and care. Address yourselves to that one thing; at any cost have this transcendent character exchanged for yours.[4]

Henry Drummond

Love Imparted

8. As you review this chapter, ask the Lord what He wants you to learn concerning the character of love. Is there a verse on which you need to meditate or a teaching about which you need to pray so that His love can begin to dwell in your heart in a more powerful way? Write down your thoughts and pray for God's love to invade your heart and teach you about what you personally need to become a woman who loves.

℘ Scripture Memory Verses:

1 Corinthians 13:4–7

CHAPTER 6

LOVING THE SAINTS

✙

*So accept each other just as Christ has
accepted you; then God will be glorified.*
Romans 15:7 NLT

When God was merciful, when He revealed Jesus
Christ to us as our Brother, when He won our hearts
by His love, this was the beginning of our instruction
in divine love. When God was merciful to us, we
learned to be merciful with our brethren. When we
received forgiveness instead of judgment, we, too, were
made ready to forgive our brethren. What God did to
us, we then owed to others. The more we received, the
more we were able to give; and the more meager our
brotherly love, the less were we living by God's mercy
and love. Thus God Himself taught us to meet one
another as God has met us in Christ.[1]

Dietrich Bonhoeffer

*S*ince love is the supreme gift to receive and to give, Jesus has commanded, not just recommended, that we love one another as He has loved us. His love was sacrificial and selfless; this is the kind of love we are give to others. The good news is that the source of our love is from God Himself, and it becomes ours as we abide in Christ and obey His commands. Jesus wants His saints to bear the fruit of love especially to the body of Christ, for it sends a powerful message to the world that we belong to Him. This body of believers is distinctive and knitted together according to His purposes in order to accomplish His will in the church and ultimately in the world.

The Body of Christ

1. The Bible speaks of the children of God who compose His family as "saints." What distinguishing characteristics of this family or body of believers are found in the following verses?

    a. 1 Corinthians 12:12–14

    b. Ephesians 2:19–22

c. Colossians 1:15–18

2. The body of Christ is uniquely fashioned to work together. What insights can you find in the following passages about God's purpose for His body and how He has equipped it to function?

a. Romans 12:3–8

b. 1 Corinthians 12:4–11

c. Ephesians 4:11–16

Christians are not independent of each other: *they should not seek to be so.* We are not the body of Christ *individually*, but we are *collectively*. We are not set to stand alone, but with others. We can help others and be helped ourselves. Another's work may be needful for the success of ours, ours for the success of another's. One supplies just what the other lacks. So that if all supply what they can, the body becomes perfect in working.[2]

H. Bremner

3. God equips each of His children with gifts so they can serve. As you have been a part of a body (e.g., church, Bible study, fellowship meeting), what one or two observations can you make concerning how different members build up one another?

Love for the Body

4. Christ is the head of the body, and His Word describes how we should conduct ourselves with one other. What do the following Scriptures teach about how we are to relate within the body?

a. Ephesians 4:1–6

b. Colossians 3:14–15

c. 1 Peter 4:7–11

d. 1 John 4:20–5:1

5. All of these exhortations encourage us to express love for other Christians. Which verse or verses challenge you the most in terms of the command to love others? Why?

> You love God as much as the one you love the least.[3]
>
> *John J. Hugo*

Author's Reflection

I am always amazed to see the body of Christ at work. There are those dear people who organize a variety of activities: Sunday school classes, banquets, hospitality committees, vacation Bible school. They enjoy the challenge, they have a great ability to motivate others to help, and they are good at seeing the overall picture. This is definitely a gift from the Holy Spirit to serve the church.

I do not have this gift. It would be extremely stressful for me to organize anything! Often I observe others quietly cleaning up after a meeting. It seems to be natural for them to see the need and begin to serve in this way. I think, *I should be helping them,* but I'm usually over in a corner exhorting someone!

It is encouraging to see how God has knit us together for the good of the whole body. Now, in order for me not to feel envious ("I'm not the committee chairman"), or guilty ("I'm not always the first to start washing dishes"), I need to understand that Christ is the head of the body and the Holy Spirit bestows the gifts as He purposes. It is *God's* church, not mine!

Essentially, what the Lord wants me to do above all else is to love other Christians fervently. In loving them, I am motivated to use my gift, and the body is blessed. When I do love and serve, I promote unity and God is glorified.

It all sounds good and right to love the body, but the church is composed of individuals who, for me, are not always easy to love *fervently*. I think Peter wrote from his own experience with the church when he said, "Most important of all, continue to show deep love for each other, for love covers a multitude of sins" (1 Peter 4:8 NLT). And the apostle John does not mince words—"And God himself has commanded that we must love not only him but our Christian brothers and sisters, too"(1 John 4:21 NLT).

Again I'm reminded that love is the supreme gift and that loving the saints is really a matter of obeying Christ's command; it is a choice I must make if I say I love God.

How can I fulfill this command to love passionately, gently, and patiently? Perhaps I need to continually revisit the Vine, strengthening and deepening my connection to the Source as I take on the character of love.

> Sanctification means the impartation of the Holy qualities of Jesus Christ. It is His patience, His love, His holiness, His faith, His purity, His godliness, that is manifested in and through every sanctified soul.[4]
>
> *Oswald Chambers*

Love Imparted

6. As you review this chapter, ask the Lord what He wants you to learn concerning loving the saints. Is there a verse on which

you need to meditate or a teaching about which you need to pray so that His love can begin to dwell in your heart in a more powerful way? Write down your thoughts and pray for God's love to invade your heart and teach you about what you personally need to become a woman who loves.

 Scripture Memory Verse:
Romans 15:7

#

$\mathcal{L}$OVE

IN $\mathcal{A}$CTION

Dear children, let us stop loving with words or lips, alone, but let us love with actions and in truth.

1 John 3:18 WILLIAMS

Compliments and flatteries become not Christians; but the sincere expressions of sacred affection, and the services or labours of love, do.[1]

Matthew Henry

$\mathcal{S}$tudying the Scriptures to understand God's great love has shown us what supreme value God places on love. We have gotten glimpses of Jesus' love, of His compassion for others, of His love for us. His words on the night of His betrayal comprised truths straight from His heart to His close disciples. During that time, He shared a new command—a fitting admonition from the Son of God to His followers—"I want you to love one another as you have seen Me love." It is indeed an encouragement to read and study about this love, but it is not enough just to think about it or discuss it. This declaration demands action, not a weak verbal response. Love that actively demonstrates the sacrificial love of Christ is what the Lord desires.

Loving in Deed

1. We have studied how Jesus showed compassion to others by ministering to them in tangible ways. What instruction and encouragement can you find in the following passages about how to express love?

    a. Romans 12:9–13

b. Hebrews 13:1–3

c. 1 John 3:17–18

2. There are innumerable ways that love can be conveyed to others. There are conditions, though, on the kind of love that should be communicated. What do the verses below reveal about what needs to be present in our lives when we minister to others?

a. 1 Corinthians 13:1–3

b. Colossians 3:17

c. 1 Peter 1:22

3. Just because we do something good for someone doesn't necessarily mean that we have done it in a way that brings glory to God. What personal needs might underlie your attempts to love others for your own benefit instead of for God's glory?

When the self knows that it is already accepted, unconditionally, there is no need anymore for it to preoccupy itself with advancing its own claims or with trying to create the conditions that might make it worthy of being loved. As long as the self is consumed in the struggle to make itself lovely, it cannot love. First it must come to the end of its own resources, for the power to love drives purely and solely from the knowledge that one is already loved in return. The energy for love flows not out of any effort, but simply from being loved.[2]

Mike Mason

Loving in Truth

4. Truth incorporates authenticity, genuineness, righteousness, and integrity. Certainly our expressions of love should be genuine,

but because all Christians have different abilities and are at various stages of maturity, the Scriptures address some of the concerns that can make it difficult to love in truth. Study what Paul taught in Romans 14:1–15:3 about relating to one another, and write down his instructions.

5. Under the influence of the Holy Spirit, Paul wrote these words in Romans (14:1–15:3) to avoid potential problems in the church. How do you see these same issues affecting the church today?

Author's Reflection

Essentially, love in action means laying down our lives. To lay down means to give up, to relinquish, to surrender. It means considering the needs of others above my own, proactively looking to see if my brothers or sisters are in need. It means walking in the Spirit so that I can listen to and obey His promptings to love.

How often I've been with people, listening to them tell what is happening in their lives, and when it time for us to part, I give a quick hug and a smile and send them off. It's usually afterward that I realize there were several ways I could have expressed genuine love to them. Most importantly, I could have prayed with them—whatever their circumstances.

From this chapter, I come away with a deeper conviction to pray—for a fervent love, a sacred affection, a pure heart, a sensitivity to the needs of the saints, a tender spirit, a courteous manner. Perhaps as I pray and abide in Christ, then causing another to stumble will not be an issue in my life. Perhaps as I pray and abide in Christ, then the little I do will be done in truth and in the name of the Lord Jesus. Perhaps as I pray and abide in Christ, I will be able to lovingly and willingly lay down my life—just as Jesus did for me.

This is how we've come to understand and experience love: Christ sacrificed his life for us. This is why we ought to live sacrificially for our fellow believers, and not just be out for ourselves. If you see some brother or sister in need and have the means to do something about it but turn a cold shoulder and do nothing, what happens to God's love? It disappears. And you made it disappear.

1 John 3:16–17 MESSAGE

Love Imparted

6. As you review this chapter, ask the Lord what He wants you to learn concerning how to love in deed and in truth. Is there a verse on which you need to meditate or a teaching about which you need to pray so that His love can begin to dwell in your

heart in a more powerful way? Write down your thoughts and pray for God's love to invade your heart and teach you about what you personally need to become a woman who loves.

 Scripture Memory Verse:
1 John 3:18

$\mathcal{L}$OVE
$\mathcal{F}$ORGIVES

*Be gentle with one another, sensitive. Forgive
one another as quickly and thoroughly as
God in Christ forgave you.*

Ephesians 4:32 MESSAGE

Given the reality of sin, love and forgiveness are inextricably bound together. God is continually, literally, second-by-second covering our sin under His Son's blood and forgiving us our sins. God cannot love us unless He forgives us and cannot forgive us without a commitment to love us. Love and forgiveness are equally bound together in all human relationships. I cannot hope to ever love someone unless I am committed to forgive him. I cannot hope to ever forgive him— that is, truly forgive him—unless I know the rich, incomprehensible joy of being forgiven.[1]

Dan Allender

*F*orgiveness runs counter to human nature. When we have been hurt, we want others to feel the hurt that has stung us. But if we are intent on learning to love as Jesus loved, then we must embrace and practice the loving act of forgiveness. Jesus' death made possible *our* forgiveness and reconciliation. "In Him we have redemption through His blood, the forgiveness of sins, according to the riches of His grace" (Eph. 1:7 NKJV). Since the Lord extended His grace and forgiveness to us, so must we give grace and forgiveness to others—loving as He loved. The "forgiveness" part of love is one of the facets of love that makes it supreme. True love forgives—it pardons, bears no grudge, covers a multitude of sins, does not take into account a wrong suffered. Forgiveness is rarely easy, but it is always right.

God's Forgiveness to Us

1. The obedient Suffering Servant, the Lord Jesus, was wounded for our transgressions. Record two or three of your primary impressions concerning the Lord's sacrifice as you meditate on the prophetic passage in Isaiah 53.

2. God's mercy to us is as high as the heavens are above the earth. What do the following passages reveal about how God views our sin?

    a. Psalm 103:10–14

    b. Psalm 130:3–4

3. Sometimes we feel justified in withholding forgiveness. But that is not the way God treats us. What can the following passages teach us about God's mercy and grace to us?

    a. Isaiah 43:25

    b. Romans 3:21–26

    c. Colossians 3:12–13

4. Our reluctance to forgive might be an indication that we have not fully received God's pardon. How has your experience of God's forgiveness influenced your forgiveness of others?

I sometimes hear people say, "I forgive him—I just don't want to have anything to do with him again." This statement always makes me think of the part of the Lord's Prayer that says, "forgive us our debts, as we also have forgiven our debtors" (Matt. 6:12). Therefore, I will often respond to this kind of statement by asking, "What would happen if God forgave you in exactly the same way you are forgiving this other person? To put it another way, how would you feel if you had just confessed your sin to the Lord and then heard his voice saying, 'I forgive you—I just don't want to have anything to do with you again'?" Most people quickly agree that they wouldn't feel the least bit forgiven. As Christians, we cannot overlook the direct relationship between God's forgiveness and our forgiveness.[2]

Ken Sande

Our Forgiveness to Others

5. God asks us to rise above our human tendencies in responding to people who hurt us. How does God's Word in Romans 12:17–21 teach us to deal with others' iniquities in a Christlike way?

6. Unforgiveness can be so destructive to our own lives that Jesus adds a "p.s." to the Lord's Prayer to warn us about it, in Matthew 6:14–15.

As the writer of Proverbs asserts, "runaway emotions corrode the bones" (14:30 MESSAGE). What does Jesus teach in the following passages about the importance of forgiving others?

a. Matthew 6:9–15

b. Matthew 18:21–35

7. Jesus' teaching on forgiveness places a clear and definite condition on our forgiving others. What are some ways in which an unforgiving spirit can affect your relationship with the Lord?

The person who accepts forgiveness becomes deeply aware of his own weakness and need. Pride is ruled out as we take our place as supplicants before the Lord. This basic attitude releases us from our tendency to become angry with, or judgmental of, others . . . [We] are freed to respond as God does, with loving concern and forgiveness. It isn't that God will not forgive the unforgiving. It is simply that the unforgiving lack the humble attitude that both permits them to accept forgiveness and frees them to extend forgiveness.[3]

Lawrence O. Richards

Author's Reflection

We are not to take lightly the Scripture that asks us to put away bitterness, wrath, and anger. If we don't relinquish bitterness, this strong emotion can destroy us from within.

I have come to understand that forgiving others is first and foremost for *my* good. Releasing others frees me from the devastating effects of holding onto anger and hurt. Whether the other person receives my forgiveness is not the major issue; what is important is that I extend forgiveness in obedience to the Lord.

I believe that the Lord loves me with a love that seeks only what is ultimately best for me. Because I love the Lord and desire to please Him, I want to do what He asks. As a forgiven child, I know that my heavenly Father will take vengeance and repay those who deserve it. Forgiveness does not mean that the perpetrator goes free; it means that the *forgiver* is free and that God will justly deal with those who have caused pain.

Forgiveness forged by love can radically change the forgiver. In this act of obedience I let go of the *me* who hurts, who wants to retaliate, who desires the other person to suffer as I have suffered. When I forgive, something extraordinary begins to take root in my soul, something fresh and new, something that makes me feel I am somehow stronger. For once I have done something that is counter to my *self* and though it doesn't seem logical, I know in my heart that it is right.

Could it be that the Lord God knows best? Could it be that to love and to forgive others blesses and enlarges the heart and soul of the lover and forgiver? And could it be that when we obey the Lord's command to love as He loved, to forgive as He as forgave, that we receive abundantly more than the little that we are asked to give?

Forgiveness is not a feeling. Neither is it simply trying to forget the bad things done to us. It is an act of the will and heart. It is giving a person something they have not earned the right to have—pardon. Forgiveness acknowledges that we have been wronged but it goes beyond that and extends mercy.

Sometimes forgiveness is a process. If we have been deeply hurt, it takes time for the wound to heal. In this case forgiveness acts as a continual cleansing of the wound so that it can heal properly. As we think about a person who has hurt us or sinned against us, feelings of resentment and emotional pain well up. Then we must reaffirm our commitment to forgive them. It is not that the first act of forgiveness was invalid, but that an ongoing process may be necessary until we are completely healed.[4]

Floyd McClung

Love Imparted

8. As you review this chapter, ask the Lord what He wants you to learn concerning forgiveness. Is there a verse on which you need to meditate or a teaching about which you need to pray so that His love can begin to dwell in your heart in a more power-

ful way? Write down your thoughts and pray for God's love to invade your heart and teach you about what you personally need to become a woman who loves.

 Scripture Memory Verse:
Ephesians 4:32

CHAPTER 9

$\mathcal{L}$OVE
$\mathcal{R}$ECONCILES

If you are in the act of worship and become aware that your actions have caused hurt, anger, resentment, or wounded feelings in another, your awareness requires initiative. Stop your acts of worship and make your best effort to restore peace and friendship by humbling yourself and accepting responsibility for the effects of your actions. Then continue your worship.[1]

PARAPHRASE OF MATTHEW 5:23–24

We must not bring malice and hatred into the temple of the Lord; we cannot worship aright while we cherish wrath in our heart. For he is love, and the unloving cannot serve him acceptably. He will not accept the offerings of those who live in strife. Malice and envy rob the gift of all its value. Forgiveness of injuries, sorrow for our own offences, the humble petition for pardon from any whom we may have offended, is a sacrifice well pleasing unto God.[2]

B. C. Caffin

*R*estoration and unity are of supreme importance to God, who went all the way to the cross to reconcile us to Himself and thereby to one another. A forgiving heart desires to remove any hindrance that might exist in a relationship. When we worship the Lord, He looks for a pure and loving heart behind our offering. Desire for unity, a willingness to humble ourselves, and a merciful heart honor and please the Lord.

Reconciliation involves acceptance, deference, peacemaking, and restoring harmony. Psalm 133:1 (NKJV) says, "Behold, how good and how pleasant it is for brethren to dwell together in unity." It is the good and pleasant—a reconciled body of believers—that love promotes.

The Call of Reconciliation

1. If the body of Christ is to function as God desires, harmony among its members is vital. What do the following Scriptures teach about our responsibility in fostering unity?

a. 2 Corinthians 5:17–21

b. Philippians 2:1–3

c. Hebrews 10:24–25

Love works wisely and gently in a soul where he wills it, powerfully extinguishing short temper, envy, and all passions of anger and self-pity, bringing into the soul in their place the virtues of patience, mildness, peaceability, and warmth toward one's fellow Christians.[3]

Walter Hilton

2. The writer of Hebrews exhorts Christians to "consider one another in order to stir up love and good works" (10:24 NKJV) within the body. What are some ways in which you might "stir up" love and good works to maintain harmony in your community of believers?

The Practice of Reconciliation

3. In the Sermon on the Mount, Jesus identifies our personal tendencies to be critical of others while overlooking our own faults. What instruction does Jesus give in Matthew 7:1–5 that can help us in practicing reconciliation?

> **Thus the passage as a whole does not say that we never ought to try to remove such "motes," but that this is monstrous and almost impossible so long as we ourselves have a fault of so much magnitude as censoriousness.**[4]
>
> *A. Lukyn Williams*

4. Because hurts and misunderstandings will occur within the body of Christ, the Scriptures teach us how to restore relationships. As you study the following Scriptures, fill in the appropriate columns.

Scripture	Method of Dealing with the Offense	Person Responsible for Reconciliation
a. Matthew 5:21–24		

Scripture	Method of Dealing with the Offense	Person Responsible for Reconciliation
b. Matthew 18:15–17		
c. Galatians 6:1–5		
d. 1 Peter 4:8		

Although it is often best simply to overlook the sins of others, there will be times when doing so only prolongs alienation and encourages them to continue acting in a hurtful manner. If you know that someone has something against you, go to that person and talk about it even before you worship God. Moreover, if another person's sins are dishonoring God, damaging your relationship, hurting others, or hurting that person, one of the most loving and helpful things you can do is to lovingly show that sinner where there is a need for change. With God's help and the right words (including your own confession), such a conversation will often lead to restored peace and stronger relationships.[5]

Ken Sande

5. Peacekeeping can be a strong preventive against the need for reconciliation. What are some of the truths in these Scriptures that can help us keep the peace?

    a. Zechariah 8:16–17

    b. Ephesians 4:29

    c. 1 Peter 3:8–12

Therefore, spiritual love proves itself in that everything it says and does commends Christ. It will not seek to move others by all too personal, direct influence, by impure interference in the life of another. It will not take pleasure in pious, human fervor and excitement. It will rather meet the other person with the clear Word of God and be ready to leave him alone with this Word for a long time, willing to release him again in order that Christ may deal with him. It will respect the line that has been drawn between him and us by Christ, and it will find full fellowship with him in the Christ who alone binds us together.[6]

Dietrich Bonhoeffer

6. Reconciliation is a sacred act of love and obedience. What hindrances to reconciliation can you identify in your life?

Author's Reflection

Reconciliation certainly is a sacred act of love and obedience. My initial response to conflict is to hide and hope the discord will disappear. I will rationalize that perhaps the other person really wasn't aware of or hurt by my insensitivity. But I have found that if someone's name keeps slipping into my thoughts while praying or worshiping, then I know I need to go that person and be reconciled.

I have learned that when I obediently and humbly ask for forgiveness and for restoration, I sense a deeper intimacy with the Lord and usually a stronger bond with the one I offended. But there will be times when the one offended does not want to be restored. A verse that has helped me concerning difficult relationships is Romans 12:18, "Do your part to live in peace with everyone, as much as possible" (NLT). I am responsible to do my part, but I am not accountable for the response of the other person.

It is the prompting of the Lord that I depend on to know when to overlook an offense or when to go to someone to ask forgiveness. I like what Charles H. Brent observed, "Intercessory prayer might be defined as loving our neighbor on our knees."[7] Through abiding in the Word and spending time in prayer, I can look for God's faithful leading to indicate how I should respond in restoring a relationship and how to speak only what is necessary for the building up of the body. Then my part is to obey lovingly and do all I can to uphold what is good and pleasant in the body of Christ.

Love Imparted

7. As you review this chapter, ask the Lord what He wants you to learn concerning reconciliation. Is there a verse on which you need to meditate or a teaching about which you need to pray so that His love can begin to dwell in your heart in a more power-

ful way? Write down your thoughts and pray for God's love to invade your heart and teach you about what you personally need to become a woman who loves.

 Scripture Memory Verses:
Matthew 5:23–24

CHAPTER 10

Loving Words

❦

But we are meant to hold firmly to the truth in love,
and to grow up in every way into Christ, the head.

Ephesians 4:15 PHILLIPS

Out of the abundance of the heart the mouth speaketh.
Out of a heart that is perfect towards God, in which the
love of God is shed abroad, in which Christ dwelleth,
the tongue will bring forth words of truth and upright-
ness, of love and gentleness, full of beauty and of blessing. God wills it. God works it. Let us claim it.[1]

Andrew Murray

*F*or me, the old saying, "Sticks and stones may break my bones, but words will never hurt me" is not true. Unfortunately, I can still remember some hurtful words said long ago. Words said thoughtlessly and in anger can cut deep into another's soul. James describes the tongue as "a small thing, but what enormous damage it can do" (James 3:5 NLT). If we are to love as Jesus loves, our tongue must be under control. It is out of the abundance of our heart that the mouth speaks (Matt. 12:34), so it is essential that love dwells abundantly in our hearts. Kind, gentle, considerate, truthful words can only spring from a heart abiding in Christ.

Thoughtful Speech

1. So often I have wished that I could retract many of the words I have spoken thoughtlessly. Look up the following Scriptures and record their insights on how to prevent hurtful words.

a. Proverbs 10:19

b. Proverbs 11:13

c. Proverbs 15:1

d. Proverbs 15:28

e. Proverbs 18:13

f. Proverbs 29:20

When you've got a word on the tip of your tongue, it's sometimes as well to leave it there.[2]

2. Thoughtful speech involves making some decisions about what is "off-limits" when conversing with others. What do these Scriptures teach about what we should avoid in our conversations?

    a. Ephesians 4:31

    b. Philippians 2:14

    c. Titus 3:1–2

    d. James 4:11–12

> We cannot avoid forming opinions of our fellowmen, but these should not be unjust or unkind; and, whether good or bad, opinions need not always be expressed. It is the love of finding fault which James here rebukes (James 4:11).[3]
>
> *Charles R. Erdman*

3. The Scriptures clearly state several ways to keep from hurting others by our words. Choose two or three examples, either positive or negative, of things you have spoken recently to another person. How well did your words reflect thoughtful speech?

Truthful (but Difficult) Speech

4. Speaking the truth can sometimes mean speaking words of reproof. This message is often misunderstood as condemnation and censure. There is an archaic definition of "reprove" no longer current in our usage, but I like it for its biblical accuracy: to "convince" and "convict." This understanding carries a positive connotation of encouraging someone to get back on the right path. What does Paul's description in Ephesians 4:14–16 reveal about the purpose of speaking difficult truths?

5. Admonishing another believer takes courage, discernment, and great love. The following Scriptures give encouragement to reprove and to restore a Christian who is transgressing. Write down the guidelines and principles found in these verses concerning reproof.

a. Proverbs 9:8

b. Proverbs 27:5–6

c. Luke 17:3–4

6. In the verses below, there are some good reminders for the one speaking words of reproof. Write down the necessary qualities for one who speaks the truth in love.

a. Proverbs 15:4

b. Romans 15:14

c. Ephesians 5:18–21

d. Colossians 3:16–17

> The best confronters are usually people who would prefer not to have to talk to others about their sin but will do so out of obedience to God and love for others . . . if you believe that the Bible contains authoritative instruction from God, and if you have a genuine love for God and for your brother, you will not shirk your responsibility to confront that brother in appropriate ways to help keep his life in line with God's standards.[4]
>
> *Ken Sande*

7. Truth and love must go hand in hand. What can you do differently to ensure that your speech is thoughtful and truthful, for the purpose of building others up in love?

Author's Reflection

It has been a practice of mine over the years to meditate on one verse of Scripture for an entire year. Each verse is chosen because of a specific need in my life—an area that needs conforming to the image of Christ. As I look back over the verses I have prayed over, I realize that about every other year the verse is always on the tongue! James says it well, "And so blessing and cursing come pouring out of the same mouth. Surely, my brothers and sisters, this is not right!" (James 3:10 NLT). How can I be somewhat kind in one moment and unkind in the next?

The proverb that has helped me the most in this area is Proverbs 15:28: "The godly think before speaking; the wicked spout evil words" (NLT). If I could only learn to think before I speak, then perhaps I would at least avoid spouting out unloving words.

One time my husband, Jack, and I were talking about some needed remodeling in our home. He commented that he wished he were as gifted as his brother-in-law when it came to being a handyman around the house. I was getting ready to say flippantly and teasingly, "Well, maybe my next husband will be talented in that area!" But, thanks be to God, I *thought* before I spoke. Instead my reply to him was, "Honey, I love you because you build into the lives of men." I share this incident because it is one of the few I can recall where I really did think before I spoke. Thinking before speaking truly or actually works!

My verse for this year?—James 3:17 (NKJV). Part of it

encourages me to be "peaceable . . . gentle . . . full of mercy"—good words for speaking the truth in love.

If I can enjoy a joke at the expense of another; if I can in any way slight another in conversation, or even in thought, then I know nothing of Calvary love.[5]

Amy Carmichael

Love Imparted

8. As you review this chapter, ask the Lord what He wants you to learn about speaking the truth in love. Is there a verse on which you need to meditate or a teaching about which you need to pray so that His love can begin to dwell in your heart in a more powerful way? Write down your thoughts and pray for God's love to invade your heart and teach you about what you personally need to become a woman who loves.

Scripture Memory Verse:
Ephesians 4:15

$\mathscr{L}$OVE $\mathscr{N}$EVER $\mathscr{F}$AILS

Love never fails.
1 Corinthians 13:8a NKJV

There is nothing so aggressive in the moral world as love. Man can stand before anything sooner than love. As a sustaining, resisting, aggressive power, love will "never fail."[1]

David Thomas

*T*here's a little saying that's often heard these days to sum up a subject with the brief but sweeping commentary, "it's all about . . ."—for example, "it's all about me," or "it's all about money," or "it's all about winning." It seems appropriate to say as we conclude this study, "it's all about love." Essentially this is what Jesus meant when He summarized all the commandments in one new one—loving one another as He has loved us. We've studied the supremacy and the heart of love, and we have learned that no matter what we do, if it is not done with love, our actions are unprofitable from an eternal perspective. God, who is love, wants His children to love one another so that those in the world can see and experience firsthand the love that God has shed abroad in our hearts. Love is to reign supreme in the church and to be extended to all we meet. "It's all about love," first and last: because love never fails.

The Testimony of Love

1. One of the purposes of the new commandment is that love among Christians would be evident to the world around them. What do these verses teach about the kind of impact we should have on the world?

   a. Matthew 5:16

b. John 17:20–21

c. 2 Corinthians 5:18–19

d. Titus 3:8

2. Jesus prayed that the church would be united in love, because only through love can believers build one another up and maintain harmony. What do the following passages tell us about those who cause discord within the body?

a. Proverbs 6:16–19

b. Romans 16:17–19

c. 1 Timothy 1:3–7

Let the Church be true to its high call-ing; so shall the glory of the indwelling Christ shine through it upon the dark world, draw-ing all men to him. Upon every section of the Church, and every individual member of the body, according to its measure, this responsibility rests.[2]

J. Waite

3. Many years ago I remember singing the song, "And they'll know we are Christians by our love." What are some ways in which the world can see that we love one another, and by that love be drawn to the gospel?

The Power of Love

4. God's love has the power to keep us close to Him for eternity and close to one another in the body of Christ on earth. What do the following verses reveal about the blessings of abid-ing in God's love?

a. Zephaniah 3:17

b. Romans 15:5–7

c. 1 Peter 1:3–9

5. The command to love as Jesus loves calls for consecration and perseverance. As you read through the comforting truths in Romans 8:35–39, describe the powerful nature of God's unfailing love.

6. Overwhelming victory is ours through Christ, who loves us. Review your study of the Scriptures, and describe the key biblical truths that give you confidence as you seek to become a woman who loves.

Even as the whole Christian life, so love has its two stages. There is love seeking, struggling, and doing its best to obey, and ever failing. And there is love finding, resting, rejoicing, and ever triumphing. This takes place when self and its efforts have been given into the grave of Jesus, and His life and love have taken their place. The birth of heavenly love in the soul has come. In the power of the heavenly life, to love is natural and easy. Christ dwells in the heart; now we are rooted and grounded in love, and know the love that passeth knowledge.[3]

Andrew Murray

Author's Reflection

A friend told me about a young Christian wife and mother of small children who had to have major surgery. Although her husband was not a Christian, she attended a small church. When she had the operation, the women of the church began to bring meals and help out with the children. The meals and ministry did not stop after she returned home, and they continued as she was recuperating.

After a few weeks of this steady support, the husband was overcome by the love and concern that he and his family were receiving. He came to church, and he came to the Savior. He could not resist the power of love.

Love is the fabric that enfolds the body and provides warmth and comfort. This blanket of love protects against the coldness of the world and insulates from the blustery winds of hate. Its fabric is soft yet strong, and there is great beauty in its many colors and intricate patterns. It is meant to be shared, for in the sharing it covers sin and envelops all who want to know the blessings that it alone can give.

This covering of love is large enough to include all who desire its consolation yet small enough to accommodate each one personally and abundantly. To be enfolded in this blanket is to experience acceptance and healing. It neither binds nor constricts, and amazingly permits those encompassed within its folds to move in freedom.

This blanket of love cannot be bought, but it is freely bestowed by the heavenly Weaver and its durability has stood the test of the ages. It is the one and only blanket that is needed for life. Without it the soul will grow cold and hard, and all that is accomplished will ultimately profit nothing. With it the soul will experience the intensity and tenderness of God's love and will ultimately be filled with the fullness of God. This love is the greatest of all virtues: it is transforming; it is powerful; and it never fails.

If we do not show love to one another, the world has a right to question whether Christianity is true.[4]

Francis Schaeffer

Love Imparted

7. As you review this chapter, ask the Lord what He wants you to learn concerning the unfailing nature of love. Is there a verse on which you need to meditate or a teaching about which you need to pray so that His love can begin to dwell in your heart in a more powerful way? Write down your thoughts and pray for God's love to invade your heart and teach you about what you personally need to become a woman who loves.

❦ Scripture Memory Verse:
1 Corinthians 13:8a

Watch what God does, and then you do it, like children who learn proper behavior from their parents. Mostly what God does is love you. Keep company with him and learn a life of love. Observe how Christ loved us. His love was not cautious but extravagant. He didn't love in order to get something from us but to give everything of himself to us. Love like that.

Ephesians 5:1–2 MESSAGE

The Father and the Child

The Child spoke:

Father, my heart is not the same.

Good, My child; please tell Me what you have learned.

First, I realize how essential it is to Your kingdom that I love as You love. I understand that it grieves You when I do not love. I am now aware that it hinders Your body when I do not love.

Yes, My heart longs for My children to extend My love to others.

I have also learned that the only way I can receive the love that blesses is by abiding in the Vine. And the only way to produce the fruit of love is by being a faithful branch.

And how has your heart changed?

I no longer desire to live in order to *get* love. Now I now want to *give* love—*Your* love, that takes no thought for myself. Your love that heals, unifies, and transforms. I want to love as *You* love.

My child, how it pleases Me to hear your words. Be assured that nothing will ever separate you from My love. Keep yourself in My love and you will fulfill My command to love one another as I have loved you.

Notes

Chapter 1—The Supremacy of Love
1. David Thomas, in *The Pulpit Commentary*, ed. H. C. M. Spence and Joseph S. Excell (Peabody, MA: Hendrickson, n.d.) 19:431.
2. Mike Mason, *The Mystery of Marriage* (Portland, OR: Multnomah Press, 1985), 61–62.
3. From study notes on 1 Corinthians 13 in *The Nelson Study Bible: The New King James Version* (Nashville: Thomas Nelson, 1997).
4. C. S. Lewis, *The Four Loves* (San Diego: Harcourt Brace & Co., 1988), 127.
5. Henry Drummond, *The Greatest Thing in the World* (Grand Rapids: Fleming H. Revell, 2000), 29.

Chapter 2—A New Commandment
1. H. R. Reynolds, in *The Pulpit Commentary*, 17:196.
2. William M. Fletcher, *The Second Greatest Commandment* (Colorado Springs: NavPress, 1983), 49.
3. Oswald Chambers, *My Utmost for His Highest* (Westwood, NJ: Barbour & Co., 1935), 20 September.
4. Paul E. Miller, *Love Walked Among Us* (Colorado Springs: NavPress, 2001), 34.

Chapter 3—The Source of Love
1. Chambers, *My Utmost for His Highest*, 30 April.
2. Dietrich Bonhoeffer, *Life Together* (New York: Harper & Row, 1954), 23–24.
3. C. Clemance, in *The Pulpit Commentary*, 22:110.
4. Charles Wesley, "And Can It Be That I Should Gain?", in *Hymns for the Family of God* (Nashville: Paragon Associates, 1976), 260.

5. A. W. Tozer, *The Knowledge of the Holy* (New York: Harper & Row, 1961), 105.

Chapter 4—Bearing Fruit
1. Bruce Wilkinson, *Secrets of the Vine* (Sisters, OR: Multnomah Publishers, 2001), 96.
2. R. Finlayson, in *The Pulpit Commentary*, 20:285.
3. Albert Barnes, *Notes on the New Testament* (Grand Rapids: Baker, 1998), 10:140.
4. Wilkinson, *Secrets of the Vine*, 21.

Chapter 5—The Character of Love
1. Donald S. Whitney, *Ten Questions to Diagnose Your Spiritual Health* (Colorado Springs: NavPress, 2001), 43.
2. From study notes on 1 Corinthians 13 in *The Nelson Study Bible: The New King James Version.*
3. Barnes, *Notes on the New Testament*, 11:254.
4. Drummond, *The Greatest Thing in the World*, 56–57.

Chapter 6—Loving the Saints
1. Dietrich Bonhoeffer, *Life Together*, 24–25.
2. H. Bremner, in *The Pulpit Commentary*, 19:413.
3. John J. Hugo, in *Quotes for the Journey; Wisdom for the Way,* compiled by Gordon S. Jackson (Colorado Springs: NavPress, 2000), 105.
4. Chambers, *My Utmost for His Highest*, 23 July.

Chapter 7—Love in Action
1. Matthew Henry, *Commentary on the Whole Bible* (Iowa Falls: Riverside, n.d.), 6:1079.
2. Mason, *The Mystery of Marriage*, 63.

Chapter 8—Love Forgives
1. Dan Allender, *Bold Love* (Colorado Springs: NavPress, 1992), 42.
2. Ken Sande, *The Peacemaker* (Grand Rapids: Baker Books, 1991), 186–87.

3. Lawrence O. Richards, *Expository Dictionary of Bible Words* (Grand Rapids: Zondervan, 1985), 291.
4. Floyd McClung, *Learning to Love People You Don't Like* (Seattle: YWAM Publishing, 1992), 55–56.

Chapter 9—Love Reconciles
1. Paraphrase of Matthew 5:23–24 by Dave Legg, *Relational Healing Workbook* (Colorado Springs: a publication of the People Resources Team of The Navigators, 2000), 5. Used by permission.
2. B. C. Caffin, in *The Pulpit Commentary*, 15:177.
3. Walter Hilton, *Toward a Perfect Love* (Portland, OR: Multnomah Press, 1985), 150.
4. A. Lukyn Williams, in *The Pulpit Commentary*, 15:281.
5. Sande, *The Peacemaker*, 144.
6. Bonhoeffer, *Life Together*, 36.
7. Charles H. Brent, in *Joy and Strength*, ed. Mary Wilder Tileston (Minneapolis: World Wide Publications, 1929), 351.

Chapter 10—Loving Words
1. Andrew Murray, *Be Perfect* (Minneapolis: Bethany Fellowship, 1965), 124–25.
2. Anonymous, in *Quotable Quotations*, compiled by Lloyd Cory (Wheaton, IL: Victor Books, 1990), 404.
3. Charles R. Erdman, *The General Epistles: An Exposition* (Philadelphia: The Westminster Press, 1966), 48.
4. Sande, *The Peacemaker*, 138–39.
5. Amy Carmichael, *If* (Grand Rapids: Zondervan, 1972), n.p.

Chapter 11—Love Never Fails
1. David Thomas, in *The Pulpit Commentary*, 19:428.
2. J. Waite, in *The Pulpit Commentary*, 19:415.
3. Murray, *Be Perfect*, 143.
4. Francis Schaeffer, in Quotes for the Journey; Wisdom for the Way, 106.

About the Author

Cynthia Heald is an author and speaker best known to women through her bestselling Bible study series. She and her husband, Jack, are on full-time staff with The Navigators. Heald speaks frequently to women's groups nationally and internationally. She and Jack reside in Tucson, Arizona.

Other books and Bible Studies by Cynthia Heald

Becoming a Woman of Excellence
Intimacy With God Through the Psalms
Becoming a Woman of Freedom
Becoming a Woman of Purpose
Becoming a Woman of Prayer
Abiding in Christ
Becoming a Woman of Grace
Becoming a Woman of Faith
A Woman's Journey to the Heart of God
When the Father Holds You Close
In the Secret Place of the Most High

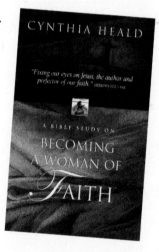

Becoming a Woman of Grace takes you on a transforming journey to the boundless reaches of God's grace. In this study guide, Cynthia Heald explores the many ways God's grace has already enriched your life and how you can know His grace more fully, and then extend it to others.

ISBN: 0-7852-7240-2

What does it mean to be a woman of faith? Is it having the right Bible verse in your back pocket or a religious quotation ready for any occasion? Cynthia Heald offers a richer perspective on the true meaning of a woman of faith. From facing challenging circumstances to being real before God, *Becoming a Woman of Faith* is a Bible study that helps women learn what it means to walk with faith in the real world and honor Christ with their lives.

ISBN: 0-7852-7244-5

In this book Cynthia Heald takes women deep into the Word to explore God's relentless, passionate pursuit of those He loves. She begins with God's question to Adam and Eve, "Where are you?" and ends with Jesus' offer, "I stand at the door and knock." In between she leads her readers into listening and responding to the words with which God earnestly seeks the hearts of His loved ones.

With strong Bible teaching, compelling insights, and personal stories, Cynthia helps women understand that these words are evidence of the Lord's great love—designed to lead them out of the trees into freedom, out of guilt into forgiveness, out of darkness into His light. Whether you are in hiding from God and others or ready to go deeper into your faith and relationships, *In the Secret Place of the Most High* will help you answer God's loving call, "Where are you?"

ISBN: 0-7852-7242-9

NOTES